ASIAPAC COMIC SERIES
● STRAT[...]

SUPREME WISDOM

◆ The Art of Insight ◆

Illustrated by **Huang Qingrong**   Translated by **Allen Zhuang**

ASIAPAC ● SINGAPORE

Publisher
ASIAPAC BOOKS PTE LTD
996 Bendemeer Road #06-08/09
Singapore 339944
Tel: (65) 392 8455
Fax: (65) 392 6455
Email: apacbks@singnet.com.sg

Visit us at our Internet home page
www.asiapacbooks.com

First published April 2000

© 2000 ASIAPAC BOOKS, SINGAPORE
ISBN 981-229-170-9

Cover design by Illusion Creative Studio
Body text in 8/9 Helvetica
Printed in Singapore by Loi Printing Pte Ltd

Publisher's Note

The founder of World Wisdom Project — an international network of professionals, thinkers, and humanitarians dedicated to mobilising the world's wisdom — Reynold Feldman believes that everyone has much wisdom to offer. Despite our cultural differences, our collective choices will determine our future.

Wisdom is a gradual process that can mature over time: we are not born wise, we *become* wise. How then do we develop our wisdom and let it well forth, so that we can make the right choices? One way is to share it with others. It is this idea that has prompted the birth of this book.

Supreme Wisdom is not about high-sounding philosophical ponderings; it is a series of short stories that depict the practicality and benefits of sagacious principles passed down from ancient China. It consolidates the wisdom of the great and the good, the eminent and the common. It is our humble wish that every reader will be inspired to develop his wisdom and contribute to the betterment of our world.

We would like to thank Huang Qingrong for the illustrations and Allen Zhuang for the translation. Our thanks also go to the production team for putting in their best efforts to make this publication possible.

Titles in the *Strategy and Leadership* series:
Supreme Wisdom: The Art of Insight
Strategies from the Three Kingdoms
Sima's Rules of War
Sun Bin's Art of War
Sunzi's Art of War
Golden Rules for Business Success
Chinese Business Strategies
Thirty-six Stratagems
100 Strategies of War
Gems of Chinese Wisdom
Three Strategies of Huang Shi Gong
Six Strategies for War
Sixteen Strategies of Zhuge Liang

About the Illustrator

Huang Qingrong 黄庆荣, also known by the name Ng Keng Yeow, was born in 1975 in Malaysia. He graduated from the One Academy of Communication Design in 1996. In 1997, he worked as an assistant to Taiwanese cartoonist Ai Leidi 艾雷迪. In the same year, he won the second prize in the Fourth Newcomer Comic Award by Sharp Point Publishing. He then came to Singapore to work with Singapore cartoonist Teo Seng Hock in the *Water Margin* comic series (six volumes) published by Asiapac Books. His other works under the *Values for Success* series include *Stories of Integrity* and *Stories of Love*. Books on supreme wisdom are in the pipeline. Huang Qingrong has also produced short comics on love and science fiction which have been serialised in a Malaysian comic magazine.

About the Translator

Allen Zhuang 庄开仁, a journalist-translator working with English and Chinese newspapers in Singapore, is keen on bridging the gap between languages and cultures. His training in comparative literature and his experience in teaching Chinese culture to Westerners came in useful during the production of this comic book for English readers.

Contents

Introduction

I make delicate efforts on the quiet, but produce effects unexpected to all.

My actions may appear conflicting but will turn out consistent; my moves may seem absurd but will prove logical.

When I appear carefree and leisurely, the smart are puzzled.

What's he up to now?

But once I've made a move, even sages can't undo it. Hey presto!

HA

I challenge you to put them all together again!

Isn't wisdom at its best when it's capable of all that?

However, Supreme Wisdom is inimitable. An aspirant might strive to attain it but still can hardly surpass the average.

For all his appearances, he's still way from it.

How come I still don't have wisdom, though I talk and move like I do?

Perhaps wisdom will just visit those lowly endowed once in a while, as the ancient saying goes.

* Supreme Wisdom

It has all these in one: Insight, Foresight, Simplicity, and Directness.

4

Handling a crisis, or tackling a task,
Wisdom works and wins, sure and fast.
To common men, this seems a puzzle;
To greater minds, as clear as crystal!

Beating Brilliance with Ignorance

After most parts of China came under the rule of the Song Dynasty, the few small kingdoms in the south pledged allegiance to the new emperor and paid tributes regularly. Southern Tang was one of the vassal states. Among its high officials were three brilliant scholars known as the Talented Xu Trio*, who were well-known even to the court of Song.

*This name came about as two of them were brothers and the third shared the same family name.

Xu Xuan stood out as the most gifted among them.

Xu Xuan was selected to head a convoy shipping Southern Tang's tribute to the court of Song. As a rule, a Song official would meet the convoy halfway and accompany it to its destination. The Song prime minister called an important meeting.

Dear fellow ministers, who of you would like to receive Xu Xuan?

Fearing to appear silly beside the brilliant Southern Tang diplomat, none of the Song ministers volunteered.

Don't pick me!

Spare me!

Not me, either!

So the prime minister had to consult the emperor.

Come see me in a while. I'll find somebody for the job.

Yes, Your Majesty!

The emperor then summoned the head court waiter and demanded a list of 10 of his subordinates who were illiterate.

When the list came, the emperor picked a name at random.

This man will do.

The ministers were taken aback by the emperor's decision.

Given no explanation or instruction, the poor court waiter set off on the mission.

The moment he received Xu Xuan on board, the latter plunged into a lengthy, eloquent talk.

Blah, blah, blah...

Unable to say anything sensible in response, the court waiter just kept nodding his head approvingly.

Xu Xuan got no clue to the scholastic or intellectual background of his counterpart. He just went on with his learned hullabaloo.

9

For days in a row during the voyage, Xu Xuan tried to engage the court waiter in conversations or debates.

The court waiter simply stayed unmoved and uninvolved. Finally, exhausted from talking, Xu Xuan had to shut up.

Just like the ancient master strategist who frustrated the enemy army without fighting a battle, the Song emperor succeeded in beating brilliance with ignorance.

Employing Each for His Forte

Han Huang served in the reign of Emperor De Zong of the Tang Dynasty as the governor-commander of Three-Wu, an area in the lower reach of the Yangtze River.

He recruited people of talent and skills and put them in posts according to their abilities.

One day, the son of an old friend came and asked for a job.

He doesn't have any special skills. What kind of job can I give him? Oh yeah, I've got an idea.

We're having a dinner party tonight. Come and join us!

Thank you. I will.

The dinner party that night turned out a grand function.

What?!

He's been sitting silently all night without a word to anyone else. What's wrong?

Oh, I see. He's a man of few words. A job in the army would suit him.

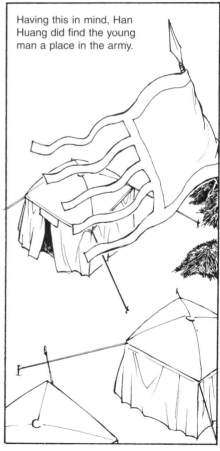

Having this in mind, Han Huang did find the young man a place in the army.

13

Because of the stern and silent guard, no soldier or official dared to come near the warehouse without authorisation.

The young man's duty was to guard the entrance to a military warehouse.

Every day, he kept guard faithfully from dawn till dusk.

Should all bosses be as observant and thoughtful as Han Huang, everybody under the sun would get employed for his forte, and no worthwhile project would be left undone.

Overlooking Others' Minor Faults

Bing Ji

Extraordinary floods are expected this year. People in areas along big rivers should be extra alert.

Bing Ji served as prime minister in the reign of Emperor Xuan of the Han Dynasty.

We must keep up preventive efforts along the dykes.

His chariot driver loved wine. One day, having drunk too much, he threw up while driving for the prime minister. The furious butler suggested firing the drunkard.

B-a-r-f!

It's nothing but a dirtied rug, isn't it? Forget it.

Well, you're the boss. It's up to you.

Now, the chariot driver was familiar with military affairs on the border, having grown up there himself.

One day, he caught sight of a courier on horseback galloping into town with a peculiar document bag.

Oh, a despatch from the border garrison! Something urgent must be happening there. Let me find out what it is.

Urgent! The Huns* have invaded several prefectures in north Shanxi!

What?

I must report to the prime minister.

* A nomadic Mongoloid tribe, also known as Xiongnu.

16

Residence of the prime minister

Are you sure?

Certainly! Some governors and commanders in those places, I fear, are too old and ill to fight back. Your Excellency may wish to look into it.

Right you are!

Immediately, Bing Ji asked to see the official-in-charge and looked into the personnel files of the border officials.

True, some are too old.

Soon, Emperor Xuan summoned the prime minister and the chief counsellor.

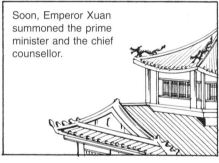

How are our governors and commanders in the invaded area? You must know well, Chief Counsellor.

Er... sorry, I'm not very sure.

As Chief Counsellor, you ought to know better. You're not fit for the post. Now, Prime Minister, do you know anything about them?

Yes, Your Majesty!

Bing Ji reported his findings and was praised for dutifully monitoring the border situation. He owed it to the timely alert of the grateful chariot driver.

Some of the border prefectures' governors and commanders are old and in poor health.

Overlook people's minor faults, and they will return your kindness with their abilities.

Putting Out a Spark Before a Fire Starts

As the prime minister, Qin Hui was at the peak of fame and power during the early decades of the Southern Song Dynasty.

How wise our Prime Minister is!

Good morning, Your Excellency!

Our Prime Minister is sooo handsome!

Eager to benefit from Qin Hui's influence, a young scholar wrote a letter of recommendation in his own favour, imitating the prime minister's handwriting.

Prime Minister Qin recommends me for a post. Hee, hee!

My art of forgery is superb. Let me go see the chief of Yangzhou prefecture with it.

Residence of the prefecture chief

Good morning, Your Excellency! Here's a letter of recommendation from the prime minister.

Let me see — what is it about?

Ah? The handwriting is suspicious!

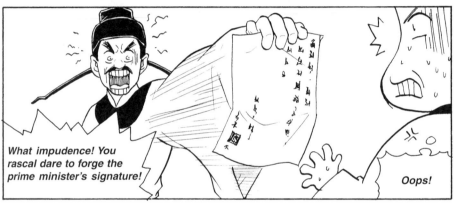

What impudence! You rascal dare to forge the prime minister's signature!

Oops!

Men, arrest the forger!

What bad luck! The letter was written perfectly.

The prefecture chief sent the culprit over to Qin Hui in the capital.

Alas, no chance for me now!

On the contrary, Qin Hui pardoned him. More surprisingly, he offered the young man a post as an official.

You're a good writer. Would you like a job with the government?

Sure!

Your Excellency, why are you so kind to that dirty cheat?

The young man must be unusually ambitious and bold since he has the guts to forge my signature...

So I need to keep him bound to our side with a post.

Considering Others' Dignity

King Zhuang of the state of Chu was a wise king in the Spring and Autumn Period. One day, he treated his officials to a grand banquet.

My pretty maid, go and serve wine to everybody!

Yes, sir!

Evening fell while the dinner party was still going on. Candles were lit.

Everybody was drunk.

Come on, one more drink!

Suddenly, the candles went out, and for a moment it was dark in the hall. One of the guests pulled at the dress of the maid.

!!

Upset and ashamed, the girl grabbed a tassel from the man's headdress, and tore it off.

I'll soon find out who the cheeky guy is!

The maid moved to a well-lit corner for a better look at the tassel.

Well, why should I humiliate an official in public just to prove the chastity of a maid?

Oh yeah, I've got an idea.

24

Hey, everybody: we're really having a good time. Let's all tear off our headdress tassels and go wild making merry!

So everybody did tear off their headdress tassels and threw them into the fire.

The dining and wining went on late into the night, when everyone had enjoyed himself to the fullest.

Years later, the Chu army fought a war against the state of Zheng. Among the many warriors of Chu, one stood out with exceptional prowess. He would cut off the enemy's head after a few bouts of fight.

After Chu won the war, King Zhuang asked about the brave fighter, who turned out to be the man who had pulled at the maid's dress that night.

A wise ruler would consider his subjects' dignity and avoid humiliating them in public. In return, he would earn their best service.

One Good Turn Deserves Another

The beginning of the Han Dynasty saw a restoration of the ancient enfeoffment system. Members of the emperor's family were given hereditary titles and land with power over their respective territories.

In the reign of Emperor Wen, Yuan Ang served as the chief minister at the court of the king of Wu, one of such lords.

One of Yuan Ang's valets had a liaison with a maid-concubine of his master.

You may wish to know, Your Excellency, that a girl of yours...

But Yuan Ang did not seem upset. Instead, he wanted to keep the affair secret.

Don't you breathe a word to anybody!

Oh sure, I won't.

Give me 100 *liang* of gold as hush money, or else...

But the informant blackmailed the valet instead.

What?! That's too much!

Fearing punishment by his master, the poor lover fled.

Farewell, my dear girl! If only I could afford the money!

Finding the young man missing, Yuan Ang gave chase and caught up with him.

Don't be afraid! I have a word for you.

Come back with me. I'll give you the girl in marriage and treat you well as before. Will that be OK with you?

A thousand thanks to Your Excellency!

Later, in the reign of Emperor Jing of Han, Yuan Ang was promoted to a high position in the imperial court, no longer serving the king of Wu. By then, some feudal lords had grown powerful and ambitious. It then happened that the emperor sent him on a mission.

At your service, Your Majesty!

You've served the king of Wu and know things there well. Go as my emissary.

Now the king of Wu was busy plotting a rebellion against the emperor. He planned to kill Yuan Ang.

You lead 500 soldiers in storming the guesthouse tonight. Make sure you kill Yuan Ang!

Yes, Your Lordship!

Fortunately for Yuan Ang, his former valet was now a captain among the troops sent to kill him.

Something must be done!

In the evening, he bought 200 jars of good wine and treated his comrades to a hearty drink. The soldiers all got intoxicated.

Great wine!

29

Handling Rules with Flexibility

In the Eastern Jin Dynasty, barbaric tribes ruled the north of China. Wang Meng served as the chief minister in the reign of Fu Jian, king of the Earlier Qin, which was one of the 16 tribal kingdoms. Now as the chief commander he was leading a 160,000-strong army in war against the Earlier Yan, another kingdom.

The Earlier Yan army, led by Murong Ping, was positioned around Luzhou in what is now Shanxi province.

The two armies faced each other outside the walled city of Luzhou.

Wang Meng summoned a general.

Yes, sir!

General Xu Cheng, you lead a detachment, go spy on the enemy and get back by midday.

But Xu Cheng did not return until dusk.

That's outrageous! The military law has death for this offence!

Zheng Qiang, Xu's superior

But the enemy outnumbers us, and we're launching an attack early tomorrow. We need people. May I ask for your pardon on his behalf?

But how am I to uphold the military law if Xu is not punished?

32

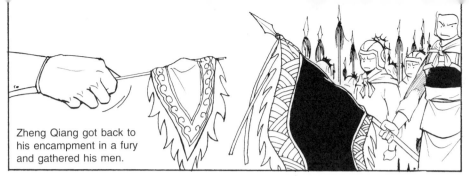

Zheng Qiang got back to his encampment in a fury and gathered his men.

All right! My troops will attack you first, Wang Meng!

Hold on! General Xu is pardoned.

I just wanted to test you, General Zheng. Since you are so faithful to your subordinate, your loyalty to our kingdom is beyond questioning.

Oh, I see!

Outwitting Thieves with a Thief

When Emperor Gao Zong of the Tang Dynasty was leaving Chang'an, the then capital, on a tour of inspection to Luoyang, a famine was at its worst in areas along his route.

Your Majesty, we need stronger security measures during the journey.

True, hungry people may turn to crime like stealing and highway robbery.

Wei Yuanzhong, the chief inspector, was assigned the task of maintaining security for the imperial entourage.

You're to clear the road and check the security. Make sure nobody is hurt and nothing is lost throughout the journey!

Yes, Your Majesty!

Embarking on the assignment, the chief inspector first visited the local county prison.

It's getting dark. I'd better hurry!

He found a man who moved and talked with an unusual air. He was serving his time for theft.

Yes, sir!

Remove his handcuffs and fetters!

Then, Wei Yuanzhong had him dressed decently and brought him back home in his own chariot.

Follow me!

OK.

36

The chief inspector invited the ex-prisoner to dine with him.

Help yourself.

Thank you very much!

And they shared a bed at night.

Z... z... z...

Then, Wei Yuanzhong entrusted him with maintaining security for the imperial entourage.

I need your help. It's like this...

Willingly, the ex-thief promised to do his best.

You've been so nice to me. I'll do all I can for you. Thank you, sir, for you've given me a new lease of life!

Praise Encourages Worthy Pursuit

Liu Pin had been an official in the capital, but later was demoted to the post of a local administrator in the backwoods of south-west China, which was a form of exile common in the Tang Dynasty.

Near Luzhou, where Liu Pin governed as the prefecture chief, there lived a young student from a police officer's family.

Ha, ha! What a brilliant essay I've composed!

But, in reality, he did not have a flair for the art of writing.

See what inspiration I've got today!

I hear a new prefecture chief has just taken office.

Why not pay him a visit and ask for his appraisal of my writings?

Oh Heavens! Exceptional! Simply wonderful!

Do you really think so, Your Excellency?

Certainly! Your essays have ingenious ideas and elegant styles, and they are refined, witty and right to the point!

Really?

Yippee!

Do keep it up, young man. Come see me again when you've new writings!

Thank you, Your Excellency, for your kindness!

Why did Your Excellency praise him so profusely? There's nothing exceptional in his writings!

Ha, ha!

Ours is a backward and uncultured place, and many youngsters end up doing evil or breaking the laws. This lad is not from a scholar's family, and yet he is keen on learning.

Staying Put to Do Good

Wang Anshi served as prime minister in the court of Emperor Shen Zong (AD 1068-1085) of the Song Dynasty. As part of a massive reform drive, he launched a series of New Deals in AD 1069.

The New Deals shall come into effect from today!

Thank you for Your Majesty's support!

Unfortunately, because of poor management, unrest started in local prefectures and counties.

No to New Deals!

I protest!

Daylight robbery!

No!

At that time, the philosopher Shao Yong was living as a recluse, declining offers of government positions.

Among his followers and disciples...

... and friends and old pals...

... were quite a few with official posts at various levels.

Most of them objected to the New Deals. They planned to write to the emperor, suggesting impeachment of the prime minister, and then resign from their posts.

44

They wrote to Shao Yong first, asking for the philosopher's advice.

They want to resign!

I must reply to each and every one of them!

Shao Yong advised them not to quit, pointing out that it was the right time for worthy officials to serve the country.

Harsh as the New Deals were, he added, the officials would do well to stay in their posts and try to lighten the burden of the common people.

Good Ethos Above Gain or Loss

Mi Buqi, a disciple of Confucius, was appointed as the magistrate of Shanfu county in the state of Lu during the Warring States Period.

Hi, guys!

Good morning, Mr Magistrate!

The state of Qi, a strong neighbouring dukedom, invaded Lu from time to time. Shanfu was situated on the route by which the Qi army advanced.

Let's pass through Shanfu.

Hearing that the Qi army was coming again, some local community leaders came and asked to see the magistrate.

The wheat is ripe in the fields. Please allow our people to harvest the crops, whether they are the owners or not.

Anyway, it would be better to obtain some food for our people than leave it for the enemy.

That's true! Please grant us permission, Mr Magistrate!

Shall I?

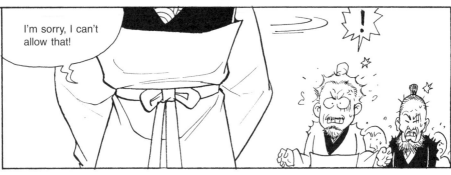

I'm sorry, I can't allow that!

The community leaders returned another three times, begging for permission.

No!

But each time they got a negative answer.

No!

No!

The Qi army did come and they did reap the wheat.

What a bumper harvest!

Jisun, the prime minister of Lu, was angry with Mi Buqi. He summoned the county magistrate and gave him a dressing-down.

Allow me to explain, Your Excellency. Even though we've lost the harvest this year, we can make up for it next year.

But if we allow our people to reap the wheat without having to toil for it, they would wish for the enemy to come again!

49

Discouraging Scandal-Hunting

Tu Pingshi served as the commissioner of education in Zhejiang province during the late years of the Ming Dynasty. He was known for strict enforcement of discipline on young scholars.

Later, he was made an inspector general of a nearby prefecture. People fond of muck-raking thought their time had come.

When a young scholar was spending a night with a prostitute, somebody gave a tip-off to a local constable, who rushed to the scene and caught them both.

Then he took them to the inspector general's office early next morning. Nobody dared to untie the pair.

The scholar violated the Code of Conduct for Scholars! He's corrupted social mores and brought shame to the community, and...

The constable knelt down and started raising a hue and cry announcing charges against them.

Pretending to see or hear nothing of the commotion, Tu Pingshi went on with his work.

Thinking that he was not loud enough to get a hearing, the constable moved forward on his knees until he came up to the inspector general.

52

Quietly, Tu Pingshi motioned to his guards to set the man and woman free.

You may go now.

Thank you!

What did you say? A scholar? Where's he?

Oh Heavens! Where's he?

The local constable received a caning for groundless accusation.

The girl was turned out of the office.

Bye, bye. Come see me some day!

He was here just a moment ago. Did I catch a ghost?

The constable was despised and shunned by other young scholars. These young men were grateful to the inspector general.

Sob...

Here's the idiot!

The trend of scandal-hunting was curbed.

The erring young scholar learnt his lesson and began to behave himself. Later he excelled in an examination and became an educational officer.

Men are apt to succumb to the lure of sex. Few talented people could be counted as perfect if judged harshly by their morals.

Seeking out their slips serves no good purpose. The wise know better than to encourage scandal-hunting.

False Accuser Deserves Punishment

In the reign of Emperor Hui Zong of the Song Dynasty, there was a young scholar who came to Kaifeng prefecture, the then capital, to sit for the imperial examinations. He was often bullied by his servant.

Ha, ha, what great fun!

Finally, the young man could not bear it any longer. He decided to take his servant to court. So he sat down to prepare a written accusation.

A servant bullying his master! Grrr!

Hey, what are you writing, buddy?

His roommate

Nothing.

Just a complaint against my mean servant, to be filed in court.

Oh, come on, why the bother, fussing over a servant's mischief?

Err...

You're right. Well, I won't sue him, then.

Still, pretending that he was the chief of Kaifeng prefecture himself passing a sentence, the young man added a line as a joke:

Sentence:
20 strokes of the cane

Come, let me treat you to a snack somewhere and you'll cool down!

All right, thanks!

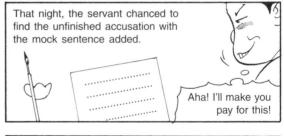

That night, the servant chanced to find the unfinished accusation with the mock sentence added.

Aha! I'll make you pay for this!

The next morning, the servant took the letter to the prefecture chief's office, and filed a suit against his master for forgery of law enforcement documents.

The young scholar was taken to court, hands in chain.

How dare you forge a court sentence in my name?

The young man recounted how he had written that complaint with the mock sentence, and why.

That's outrageous! What a mean servant!

OK, I think I'll just pronounce the sentence you gave: 20 strokes of the cane for this impudent servant!

Yes, sir!

For me?!

The servant learnt his lesson and dared not take liberties any longer.

Ouch! It hurts so!

Thank you, Your Excellency!

It is wrong to imitate a law enforcement official's writing even as a joke, but it is important that the servant know his place.

Overlooking a harmless minor offence, I focused on a more serious trespass which could eventually pose a threat to social hierarchy, and hence, the basis of the state's rule. Wisdom lies in the ability to perceive the real issue.

Don't forget who you are!

I'm the servant, master!

Ouch!

Forbearance Essential for Success

Zhang Er and Chen Yu were well-known men of talent and influence in the state of Wei — one of the major powers during the Warring States Period — even though they held no office.

I, Zhang Er, am a master strategist.

And I, Chen Yu, am a great warrior!

Then, after a series of bitter wars, Wei was destroyed by the state of Qin in 225 BC, which later brought the whole of China under its rule in 221 BC.

Fearing Zhang Er and Chen Yu would lead a resistance movement to restore Wei, the Qin ruler offered handsome rewards for information leading to their capture or death.

* 10,000 liang *of gold for Zhang Er*

** 10,000 liang *of gold for Chen Yu*

The two friends fled under false identities to the territory of the former state of Chen, which had been annihilated long before.

Here's the old Chen's capital city. Who are you?

My name is Lim Ah Beng.

I'm Tan Ah Seng.

They managed to earn a living as gatekeepers for the city.

One day, Chen Yu blundered on his job...

Grr...

His superior gave him a sound whipping for that.

And you still dare to talk back? Who do you think you are?

Chen Yu felt he could not bear it any more.

I'd rather die than swallow such humiliation!

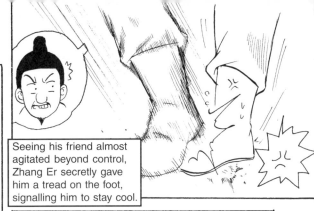

Seeing his friend almost agitated beyond control, Zhang Er secretly gave him a tread on the foot, signalling him to stay cool.

Ouch, my foot!

Goons!

Phew, he's gone!

Remember what I told you before? Bear and forbear! Would it be worthwhile if you got killed in fighting back today, or worse still, if that betrayed who we are?

Staying Off Sensual Pleasures

Emperor Wen Zong was to officiate at a ritual of sacrifice-offering to Heaven. As a rule, he was supposed to observe a purifying fast for days beforehand in a quiet place south of the city. He had to take special baths and change into clean clothes...

Abstain from wine or any other alcoholic drinks...

Eat nothing but vegetarian foods...

Refrain from moving around unnecessarily...

And, at all times, be discreet in speech and manner.

64

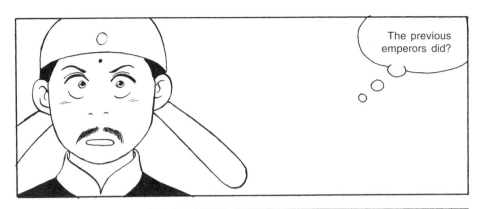

The previous emperors did?

Er... maybe the wrestlers are just expecting some tips!

Sure, they are, but...

Let them go ahead with the match outside. When they're done, just tip them as usual and let them go home.

Yes, Your Majesty!

On another occasion, a jester-actor suggested a cockfight show because, as he told the emperor, the fighter roosters were really good.

You must see them to believe!

Since you like them, I'll give them to you!

Thank you, Your Majesty!

Emperor Wen Zong refused to indulge in sensual pleasures so as to ward off those bootlicking courtiers. What is more, he handled the matter with delicacy so that his predecessors' faults were not highlighted. He is indeed a wise ruler.

Candour and Wisdom Avert Disaster

Xu Qi was the chief administrator of Guangdong in south coastal China in the reign of Emperor Cheng Zu of the Ming Dynasty. He went to Beijing for an audience with the emperor.

Stop! Here's the checkpoint. What's that in your coach, sir?

Xu Qi

Some rattan mattresses from the south, gifts for my former colleagues in the court.

May I have your list of gift recipients, sir?

Sure!

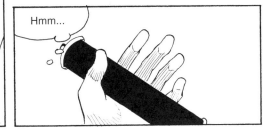

Hmm...

Suspecting some kind of conspiracy among the court officials and someone from the southern border, the officer thought he had better be wary than sorry.

I must hand it over to the emperor himself.

Here's Xu Qi's list of gift recipients.

Hmm, something dubious may be going on, judging by such a complete list of my ministers. But why is Yang Shiqi's name missing?

Emperor Cheng Zu summoned the minister in question, hoping to find out more about the list.

You alone among the court officials are missing from Xu Qi's list. Why?

!

It's like this. Not long ago, when Xu Qi was appointed to his current post, we colleagues gave him a farewell dinner party and a gift.

Thank you, my friends!

Just a memento for the years we've spent working together.

...
...

I guess Xu Qi is returning our kindness with some local products from where he works now.

And since I was the only one who missed the farewell dinner party — I was badly ill in bed then — I think that's why I am left out of the list.

Nobody knows whether those on the list will actually accept the gifts. Besides, a mattress is nothing of great worth. So I don't think there's any strange motive behind it.

I see!

His suspicion cleared, the emperor ordered that the list be destroyed.

This put an end to all suspicion and rumours about the matter and prevented consequent in-fighting, overt and covert.

With candour and wisdom, Yang Shiqi averted a disaster that would have involved many people.

I must squash this suspicion!

Using Money Judiciously

Yan Zhen served as the governor-cum-chief commander in a strategic area south of the capital in the Tang Dynasty. He was well-known for his generosity and support to charity.

Take this; you need it!

Many thanks!

Once a man came and asked him for a loan.

I understand Your Excellency are a great philanthropist.

So, may I ask for a loan of 3,000 liang of silver to start a business with?

Oh?

71

Starting a business? That's a good idea. But allow me a day or two, and I'll let you know my decision soon.

What?!

That's a huge sum, 3,000 liang of silver!

Daddy, people's ethos is really turning bad — there'll be no end to such loans. Please don't give him that!

You could bring disaster to our family — grudging money so much! You would have said the right thing by advising me to give more for charity's sake.

I'm no beggar in the street.

Besides, asking for such a big loan might mean that the man really has confidence. Perhaps he has an unusual plan or exceptional abilities.

Daddy is right!

The man was given the sum he had asked for.

Am I dreaming?

High Moral Ground Ensures Victory

Liu Bang, who later became the founding emperor of the Han Dynasty, was planning to declare war on Xiang Yu, his former ally in overthrowing the rule of Qin. He led his army into Luoyang, a strategic stronghold in central China.

At last, here's Luoyang!

Elder Dong, the head of local communities, offered his suggestion to Liu Bang.

It's common sense, Your Highness, that one must be fighting for a just cause before he can win. Prove that your enemy is in the wrong, and you will succeed.

Not long ago, when the various armies joined forces in rising against Qin, they elected Emperor Yi as the supreme leader of the alliance and all the people.

Oh?

But after Qin was toppled, Xiang Yu assumed authority and moved Emperor Yi out of the capital, relegating him to the backwoods of the south.

Clear out!

Yes, sir!

He even had him assassinated while the poor young man was on his way!

Ha, ha! Now I'm the real lord of the whole country!

Help!

To highlight Xiang Yu's crime of regicide, Your Highness should order all your troops to wear white in mourning for the murdered Emperor Yi, and denounce the culprit before all other military leaders and the people.

Liu Bang took the advice and declared war on Xiang Yu.

I, Liu Bang, ask for your support in attacking the murderer of Emperor Yi, our elected leader in overthrowing Qin!

We pledge our support!

Wonderful! I'll join forces with all my other former allies and attack the murderous Xiang Yu!

Valuing the Real Treasure

In 206 BC, Liu Bang's army took Xianyang, the capital of the Qin empire, putting an end to the despotic Qin Dynasty.

Entering the city, Liu's generals and officials rushed to the central treasury...

... and helped themselves to the gold and jewellery there.

Amid the craze, one person remained sober — Xiao He, the chief counsellor of Liu Bang.

The real treasure lies here instead!

Office of the Qin prime minister

Wow! Here are the documents and archives of Qin, all intact despite the war and unrest!

Let me see: laws and decrees, maps and statistics, reports and annals, all in good condition! Ha, ha!

Liu Bang, now the founding emperor of the Han Dynasty, had a full grasp of China's essential facts and figures — the land features, the population and their produce...

Military and strategic importance of various places...

Charge!

Oh no...

And the common people's peeves and desires.

Qin laws are cruel! Scrap them!

Taxes and duties are outrageous! Cut them!

State Interests Before Personal Grudges

By the end of the Warring States Period, Qin had emerged as the strongest state. Yet, in a summit meeting with the Qin ruler at Mianchi in 279 BC, Lin Xiangru, a Zhao diplomat, frustrated Qin's attempts to gain land from his country and humiliate his master. For his merit, Lin was appointed the senior minister, a post above Lian Po the chief general.

Lian Po had earned his post after decades of outstanding military service. He was unhappy with the new senior minister who, he thought, had gained fame and position with nothing but a glib tongue.

I'll definitely embarrass him if he crosses my path!

Hearing of the chief general's grudge, Lin Xiangru decided to avoid him.

Well, I'll just make way for him.

And he even skipped the morning conferences at court so as to avoid taking a seat more prestigious than the chief general's.

One day, seeing Lian Po coming his way, Lin Xiangru ordered his chariot driver to turn into a side street.

Hold on! We'll wait here awhile.

Your Excellency, you're too weak and easy to bully!

We're ashamed. We might as well quit!

Right!

Would you say the chief general is as formidable as the king of Qin?

Nope.

Awesome as the king of Qin is, I rebuked him in public and gave his courtiers a hearty scolding.

Now, why should I fear General Lian, a lesser terror? Qin dares not invade us precisely because General Lian and I work together. If we fought among ourselves, either he or I would be out, and Qin would benefit. I put our state's interests before personal grudges.

When Lian Po heard this, he felt terribly ashamed.

Shame on me! I've behaved like a child...

He stripped to the waist and, carrying a thorny flogging-rod on his back, had a steward lead him to Lin Xiangru's residence.

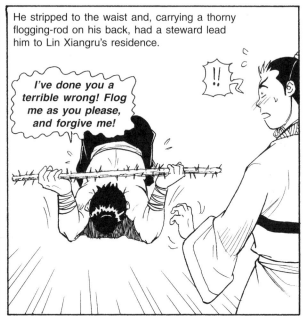

I've done you a terrible wrong! Flog me as you please, and forgive me!

They became sworn friends till death.

Putting aside personal grudges for the sake of the public interests – this is what the wise would do.

Counselling by One's Own Example

Liu Bei, the founding ruler of Shu in the Three Kingdoms Period, was keen to recruit talent for his kingdom. He welcomed Ma Chao, a brave warrior, to join his camp.

I'm at your service, sir!

Welcome! No ceremonies, please!

This is a rare talent!

Now, I appoint you as General of the West Command!

Besides, I confer the title of Marquis on you!

Thanks, sir!

Hi, Xuan De!

Seeing that Liu Bei was nice to him, Ma Chao began to take liberties by calling his master's pet name.

Guan Yu, Liu Bei's sworn brother and loyal follower, felt indignant.

What insolence! The boor has no manners at all!

Ha, ha! You're so funny, Xuan De!

Elder Brother, Ma Chao is too rude. I have a good mind to kill him!

Oh no! Please don't!

But then he...

Zhang Fei, another sworn brother of Liu Bei, had an idea.

Well, that's the rustic's way. But why not teach him proper manners with an example?

The next day, Liu Bei called a meeting of his generals and commanders. Senior Generals Guan Yu and Zhang Fei stood at attention on either side of Liu, each holding his weapon.

Ma Chao was awed when he saw them attending upon Liu Bei with deference, instead of taking their seats.

Oh, I see — my boss IS somebody! But I've been taking him lightly!

Faithfulness to Duty Earns Trust

Zhao Kuangyin was a warrior before he came to the throne in AD 960.

I used to fight on the battlefield!

Like my comrades, I fought everywhere.

In time, Zhao was promoted to the post of general commander under Emperor Shi Zong, the ruler of the Later Zhou Dynasty.

I've risen from the rank and file.

Now the army under his command was stationed in Chanzhou in central China.

How the wind howls, and how biting cold the water is!

Cao Bin

The emperor trusted Cao Bin very much.

Cao Bin, I had an interesting dream the other night. Come, I'll share it with you.

Cao was entrusted with the provision of drinks for the court.

Mind you don't get them mixed up!

This black tea is for the prime minister, and that red wine is for the chief general, and...

It's freezing cold tonight. How I wish I could get a gulp of liquor and warm up...

I've an idea! Cao Bin must have lots of good wine.

Hi, Cao Bin, you must have some wine stored away. Can you give me a drink?

Sorry, I can't, Your Excellency! It's my duty to keep it for the court's use. You'll have to buy a drink yourself, say, from a village wine shop.

Soon Zhao Kuangyin seized power in a coup and founded the Song Dynasty.

I'm the founding emperor now.

He announced to his officials:

Among those serving the previous emperor, Cao Bin alone is really faithful to his duty.

So the new emperor put his trust in Cao Bin, appointing him to a post of great responsibility in his court.

Here's a man who keeps personal ties from compromising his duty. He well deserves praise and trust.

Honesty Is the Best Policy

Lu Zongdao served as the chief counsellor in the reign of Emperor Zhen Zong of the Song Dynasty.

I'm a secret lover of wine. Hic...

One day, the emperor summoned his chief counsellor.

Go and get Lu Zongdao to come see me at once!

Yes, Your Majesty!

The messenger got to Lu's residence.

What? He's out for a drink?!

Well, then, I'll wait until he returns.

He's back at last!

I beg your pardon, sir. I've just been to a pub. Well — er — what do you want to see me about?

Humph!

His Majesty wanted you to appear in court immediately, but you've been so long in coming home.

What would you say, I wonder, if His Majesty should tell you off for keeping him waiting?

96

I think I'll just tell the truth.

Then you're sure to get punished for that!

So be it, then!

It would be a minor offence if I confessed to a weakness for wine, but telling a lie to His Majesty would be unpardonable.

The messenger returned and told Emperor Zhen Zong everything.

The emperor valued the honesty of his chief counsellor and felt sure he could be entrusted with great responsibilities.

Everyone is liable to make slips and blunders, but it would be unwise to commit grave mistakes just to cover them up.

Circumspection Leads to Precaution

Emperor Ren Zong of the Song Dynasty was once ill for a long time and could not chair the regular court conferences.

I feel terrible!

One day, he felt better and decided to meet a few chief officials at his residence.

What's been going on in the government, I wonder...

Cough! Cough!

Go and ask the prime minister and the privy councillor to come see me.

Yes, Your Majesty!

Lü Jianyi, the prime minster, made no haste to enter the palace.

Hurry up, His Majesty is waiting!

Oh?

Grr...

Wait a minute! Let me change first.

The privy councillor could not bear Lü's tarrying.

Can't you hurry up?

Damn it! He's practically taking a stroll!

I'm feeling better today and would like to see you very much.

But why have you taken so long to arrive?

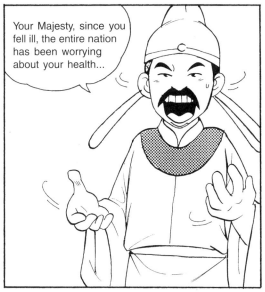

Your Majesty, since you fell ill, the entire nation has been worrying about your health...

Now that you've suddenly summoned us to a meeting, had we come rushing all the way into the palace...

Wisdom Makes Genuine Loyalty

Emperor Tai Wu of Northern Wei was leaving for a hunting exercise far away from home. He ordered Gu Bi, a senior official, to stay back in command of the garrison of Ping Cheng, the capital city, and other army units.

Don't worry, I'll take care of things.

Go back and ask Gu Bi for the best of our horses. I want them for my hunting attendants.

Sure!

But Gu Bi sent only weak and old horses over to the hunting field.

Your Majesty, Gu Bi said these are the best he could give us!

The emperor's wrath threw his officials back in the capital into panic and anxiety.

Who knows but I might get into trouble, too...

That stupid Gu Bi! He dared to disobey my order. See if I don't have him beheaded when I'm back!

Don't worry, you guys...

For those who serve a ruler, it is a minor offence if they fail to please His Majesty in entertainment...

But it would be treason if they fail in war-preparedness against aggression...

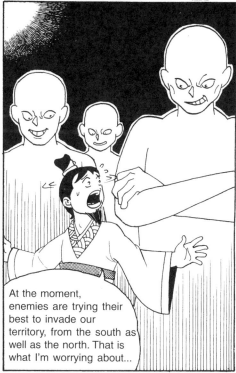

At the moment, enemies are trying their best to invade our territory, from the south as well as the north. That is what I'm worrying about...

I keep the strongest war horses for the defence of our capital and our land. I don't care if I should die for that. I alone will take the blame, if any. You're simply reproachless!

Hearing of this, Emperor Tai Wu came to see his own mistake. Instead of punishing the loyal official, he sent him a suit of ceremonial robe, a brace of horses and 10 deer as a reward.

Thank you, Your Majesty!

The emperor looked on Gu Bi as a great asset for the country. He dubbed him "Mr Upright", by which he became known.

A loyal official must have the foresight to ensure the country's security rather than please the ruler in his entertainment. Wisdom makes genuine loyalty.

To Each as He Deserves

Li Yuan, the founding emperor of the Tang Dynasty, took a stronghold from under the Sui rule.

When rewards were given out in the victorious army, some officers wanted the ex-slaves to be excluded because they had been conscripted.

Those of us from good families joined the army of our own will. Of course we should be treated differently!

We object to rewarding the ex-slaves!

We protest!

Slaves or not, we've fought together, braving the same slings and arrows. Now, when it comes to rewards, why should we stick to status?

So everybody should be rewarded as he deserves!

Sorry...

Then, Li Yuan met the soldiers and officials of the defeated city, and distributed goodies to them.

Come, you have a share, too!

Among them, he recruited some strong young men for his army.

To those who chose not to join his troops, he gave an official rank each, though without actual posts, and then let them go home.

I'm moved!

Li Yuan is nice to us.

Your Majesty, don't you think you are giving out ranks too freely?

Yeah!

Ha, ha!

The emperor of Sui grudged rewarding his men and thus lost their support. Why should I follow his example?

Weighing Advice Before Decision

During the reign of Emperor Wu of the Han Dynasty, China was often at war with Huns in the north. Wei Qing was renowned for fighting the Huns as the chief general. Now he and two assistant officers with 3,000 troops were going on yet another campaign.

I'm Wei Qing.

I'm Su Jian.

I'm Zhao Xin.

Su and Zhao met with large hordes of Hun horsemen. After a day's bitter fighting, the Chinese detachment was all but wiped out.

Zhao Xin surrendered to the Huns.

I'm willing to join you.

But Su Jian managed to return to the Chinese camp, all alone.

Zhou Ba, the adviser to the commander

Ever since the campaign started, Your Excellency have never punished a subordinate who has lost a battle...

Now, Su Jian lost all his men and came back alone. You'd be well-advised to have him beheaded to boost your severity as the chief general.

An, the secretary

No! Definitely not!

Su Jian led his troops of a few thousands in fighting tens of thousands of Huns. Our loyal soldiers fought to the bitter end...

If he were punished by death, that would be a message to others that they had better surrender to the enemy if they were defeated. No, you mustn't kill him!

I think I'll keep Su Jian in my army pending a verdict. I don't mind if I lose severity as the chief general.

So Adviser Zhou, I don't think I will take your advice.

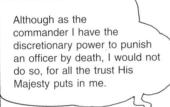

Although as the commander I have the discretionary power to punish an officer by death, I would not do so, for all the trust His Majesty puts in me.

I'd rather send him back to the capital, and let His Majesty decide...

... and let this be an example that high-level officials shouldn't arrogate power to themselves. Isn't that better?

Certainly!

Su Jian was sent back to the capital as a prisoner.

As expected, Emperor Wu pardoned him.

You're free now!

The wise listen to advice and counsel, but make their own decisions after careful consideration. Taking all circumstances into account, they act with discretion and reason.

Courtesy Is More for Ritual's Sake

In the reign of Emperor Xian Zong of the Tang Dynasty, the central government declared war on the warlords of outlying provinces who had rebelled against imperial authority. One night, General Li Su led his army in an attack on Caizhou, the power base of Wu Yuanji, a tough rebel.

Daring rebel, you're doomed tonight!

At last, the Tang army retook the walled city and captured the rebel leader.

Lock him up! He'll be taken to the capital.

Yes, sir!

Li Su then had his troops encamped and waited for Prime Minister Pei Du, who was to arrive for an inspection of the city and to announce the emperor's message to the locals.

I can see better from here.

Ah, the prime minister is coming!

Hurry up!

As Pei Du entered the city gate, General Li, in his full army outfit, knelt down by the roadside in a deep bow, ushering in the prime minister and his entourage.

Welcome, Your Excellency!

What? His Excellency shunning my bow!

...
...

Pray listen to me, Your Excellency. The locals have been under the rebels' rule for 30 years without observing proper courtesy. Please accept my bow and welcome to show them the proper rites.

Insight Detects Hidden Evil

Confucius, the great ancient sage, lived in the state of Lu during the Spring and Autumn Period. Shaozheng Mao, an official of Lu, was a contemporary of Confucius. Each had his own circle of followers and pupils.

Shaozheng Mao's followers increased steadily.

$

By contrast, Confucius's school saw ups and downs.

Not many pupils...

Later, Confucius was appointed as the police inspector general of Lu, and served in that capacity for a short time.

At last, after all these years' efforts!

He then had Shaozheng Mao condemned and executed.

Respected Master!

Yes?

Shaozheng Mao enjoyed fame across the state of Lu. Don't you think, Master, that killing him would do more harm than good?

Shaozheng Mao was guilty of them all!

He deserved death!

What's more, he had fame and position to gloss over his evils, so I couldn't allow him to go on misleading the masses.

You have a point there.

Ordinary crimes are clear to all, and rulers with a right mind can find them out. However, it takes the insight of a sage to detect evil masked by fame and position and to nip it in the bud.

Patience for Political Reason

Wang Qinruo and Ma Zhijie were fellow officials with the privy council in the reign of Emperor Zhen Zong of the Song Dynasty.

I'm Wang Qinruo.

I'm Ma Zhijie.

One day, they got into an argument over a trifling matter in the emperor's presence. They forgot all about court etiquette and polite language.

You idiot!

You silly fool!

You damn goon!

Block-head!

Wang Dan, the prime minister, witnessed the row.

I challenge you to go and have it out in the Discipline Department!

Well, good, let's go!

The emperor could not bear it any more.

Stop quarrelling, you both! Men! Throw them into prison!

Hold on, Your Majesty!

It's wrong for them to abuse Your Majesty's trust by quarrelling in court...

As leader of all officials, I ought to have them duly punished. But, Your Majesty, please calm down. I'll come again tomorrow for your instruction about this.

...
...

All right, then!

Then, Wang Dan gave the two erring officials a good telling-off. Frightened, they confessed to the violation in writing and awaited penalties.

Emperor Zhen Zong summoned the prime minister to court the next morning.

What are you going to do with those two?

They should be dismissed, but a formal charge must be found...

!?

Just this: impropriety in imperial presence!

Everyone knows Your Majesty as a wise sovereign. If our officials were dismissed for impropriety in imperial presence, the tribal vassal states might laugh at us. That is no good for Your Majesty.

125

Grasping the Essence of Etiquette

Hu Ying served in the Ministry of Rites & Examinations in the court of Emperor Ying Zong of the Ming Dynasty. One day, he attended the morning court conference.

Good morning, Your Majesty.

When he got up, his waist belt came loose.

He calmly picked up the belt, rebuckled it and kowtowed to the emperor before returning to his position, carrying himself well as required by court etiquette.

So, even the master of discipline could not impeach him for improper behaviour in court.

I must not laugh!

Pretend I didn't see it.

127

A few years later, a young scholar Peng Shi passed the imperial civil service examination and clinched the first prize.

I made it, at last!

On the eve of the all-important personal interview with the emperor, Peng Shi felt too excited to sleep. Fearing to be late the next morning, he decided to sit up till dawn.

Then, overpowered by sleep, he dozed off at around 2 am in the early morning.

Alas, he ended up missing the opening of the imperial interview. He faced impeachment for impropriety.

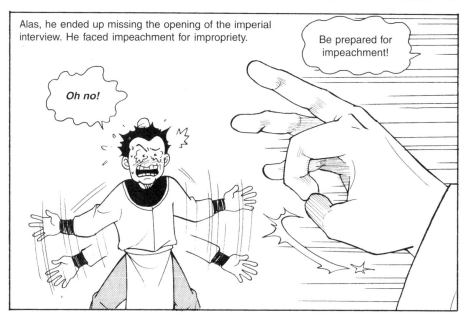

Oh no!

Be prepared for impeachment!

Since Peng Shi still had not arrived, the official-in-charge reported it to Emperor Ying Zong.

How unimaginable!

Arrest the top scholar and bring him to court!

!

Hu Ying was dismayed.

Your Majesty, in my humble opinion, it would be more proper to send the imperial guards out to find the young interviewee.

Huh?

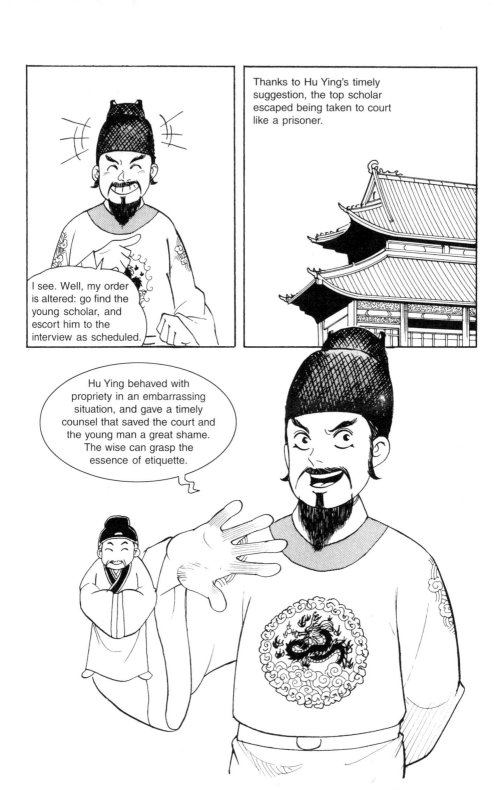

Thanks to Hu Ying's timely suggestion, the top scholar escaped being taken to court like a prisoner.

I see. Well, my order is altered: go find the young scholar, and escort him to the interview as scheduled.

Hu Ying behaved with propriety in an embarrassing situation, and gave a timely counsel that saved the court and the young man a great shame. The wise can grasp the essence of etiquette.

Charity Earns Blessings Better

Sun Jue served as the governor of Fuzhou prefecture in the reign of Emperor Shen Zong of the Song Dynasty.

Hi, I'm Sun Jue!

At that time, many poor people were in debt.

And the local prisons were full of debtors.

Poor me!

Sob... It seems I can never pay up...

133

The next day, the merchants gave the five million copper coins to the authorities. The prisons were emptied at once.

Charity earns blessings for the rich by helping the poor out of debt. But it takes the wise words of a sympathetic official to persuade those who have money.

A Brief Chronology of Chinese History

夏 Xia Dynasty			About 2100 – 1600 BC
商 Shang Dynasty			About 1600 – 1100 BC
周 Zhou Dynasty	西周 Western Zhou Dynasty		About 1100 – 771 BC
	東周 Eastern Zhou Dynasty		770 – 256 BC
	春秋 Spring and Autumn Period		770 – 476 BC
	戰國 Warring States		475 – 221 BC
秦 Qin Dynasty			221 – 207 BC
漢 Han Dynasty	西漢 Western Han		206 BC – AD 24
	東漢 Eastern Han		25 – 220
三國 Three Kingdoms	魏 Wei		220 – 265
	蜀漢 Shu Han		221 – 263
	吳 Wu		222 – 280
西晉 Western Jin Dynasty			265 – 316
東晉 Eastern Jin Dynasty			317 – 420
南北朝 Northern and Southern Dynasties	南朝 Southern Dynasties	宋 Song	420 – 479
		齊 Qi	479 – 502
		梁 Liang	502 – 557
		陳 Chen	557 – 589
	北朝 Northern Dynasties	北魏 Northern Wei	386 – 534
		東魏 Eastern Wei	534 – 550
		北齊 Northern Qi	550 – 577
		西魏 Western Wei	535 – 556
		北周 Northern Zhou	557 – 581
隋 Sui Dynasty			581 – 618
唐 Tang Dynasty			618 – 907
五代 Five Dynasties	後梁 Later Liang		907 – 923
	後唐 Later Tang		923 – 936
	後晉 Later Jin		936 – 946
	後漢 Later Han		947 – 950
	後周 Later Zhou		951 – 960
宋 Song Dynasty	北宋 Northern Song Dynasty		960 – 1127
	南宋 Southern Song Dynasty		1127 – 1279
遼 Liao Dynasty			916 – 1125
金 Jin Dynasty			1115 – 1234
元 Yuan Dynasty			1271 – 1368
明 Ming Dynasty			1368 – 1644
清 Qing Dynasty			1644 – 1911
中華民國 Republic of China			1912 – 1949
中華人民共和國 People's Republic of China			1949 –

SPECIAL OFFER

Strategy & Leadership Series in Comics

These English comics will heighten your understanding and observations of life for good decision-making and human relationships.
Educational and entertaining for the whole family.

Strategies from the Three Kingdoms

The war stratagems and military teachings which emerged from the Three Kingdoms Period have influenced the way later generations view leadership and power. These strategies are still universally relevant in today's corporate culture as well as warfare.

$12.51

Supreme Wisdom: The Art of Insight

Supreme Wisdom is part one of the classic *Gems of Chinese Wisdom*. The characters in the 32 stories here will impress you with their insight and ingenuity!

$7.88

Sima's Rules of War: The Practice of Dynamic Leadership

Famed War Minister Tian Rangju shares his experience in planning for campaigns, handling warfare, strategising for victory and much more!

$14.74

Art of War

Art of War provides a compact set of principles essential for victory in battles; applicable to military strategising, in business and human relationships.

$10.10

Sun Bin's Art of War: World's Greatest Military Treatise

The household Chinese name, Sunzi, refers to the great military strategist Sun Wu, as well as his descendant Sun Bin, who was framed and crippled but went on to win countless wars and to write the brilliant Art of War. Be inspired by his tenacity and wisdom.

$14.74

Sunzi's Art of War: World's Most Famous Military Classic

This famous military classic covers the full spectrum of strategising. Containing extensive knowledge, dealt with in great depth, it is a crystallisation of human wisdom.

$14.74

Chinese Business Strategies

Offering 30 real-life, ancient case studies with comments on their application in today's business world, this book contains tips useful to the aspiring entrepreneur.

$14.74

Golden Rules for Business Success

A collection of Tao Zhugong's principles for business success, this inspiring and penetrating book contains 12 Golden Standards and 12 Golden Safeguards.

$14.74

100 Strategies of War: Brilliant Tactics in Action
This book captures the essence of extensive military knowledge and practice, and explores the use of psychology in warfare, the importance of diplomatic ties with the enemy's neighbours, the use of reconnaissance and espionage, etc.
$14.74

Gems of Chinese Wisdom: Mastering the Art of Leadership
Wise up with this delightful collection of tales and anecdotes on the wisdom of great men and women in Chinese history like Confucius, Meng Changjun and Gou Jian.
$14.74

Thirty-six Stratagems: Secret Art of War
A Chinese military classic that emphasises deceptive schemes to achieve military objectives, this book has caught the attention of military authorities and general readers alike.
$14.74

Sixteen Strategies of Zhuge Liang: The Art of Management
With advice on how a king should govern the country, establish harmonious relations with his subjects and use reward and punishment to win his people's trust, this is a boon for those involved in business management.
$14.74

Three Strategies of Huang Shi Gong: The Art of Government
Reputedly one of man's oldest monograph on military strategy, it unmasks the secrets behind brilliant military manoeuvres, clever deployment and control of subordinates, as well as effective government.
$14.74

Six Strategies for War: The Practice of Effective Leadership
A powerful book for administrators and leaders, it covers critical areas in management and warfare. These include how to recruit talents, manage the state, beat the enemy, lead wisely and manoeuvre brilliantly.
$14.74

Note: For overseas orders, please include postage fees of S$2.50 (surface mail) for every volume ordered.

My order _____ Total: S$ _____

☐ Enclosed is my postal order/money order/cheque/for S$ _____ (No: _____)

☐ Credit card. Please charge the amount of S$ _____ to my credit card

VISA ☐ Card No. _____ Card Holder's Name _____

MASTER ☐ Expiry Date _____ Order Date _____ Signature _____

Name (Mr/Mrs/Ms) _____

Address _____
_____ Tel _____ Fax _____

Send to: **ASIAPAC BOOKS PTE LTD**
996 Bendemeer Road #06-08/09 Singapore 339944
Tel: (65) 392 8455 Fax: (65) 392 6455
Note: Prices quoted valid for purchase by mail order only. Prices subject to change without prior notice.

上智

见大

绘画：黄庆荣
翻译：庄开仁

亚太图书有限公司出版